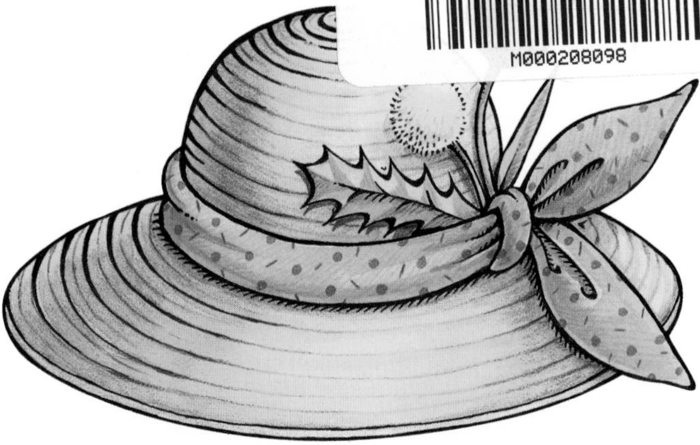

The Hat

Written by Alex Starr
Illustrated by Ruth J. Flannigan

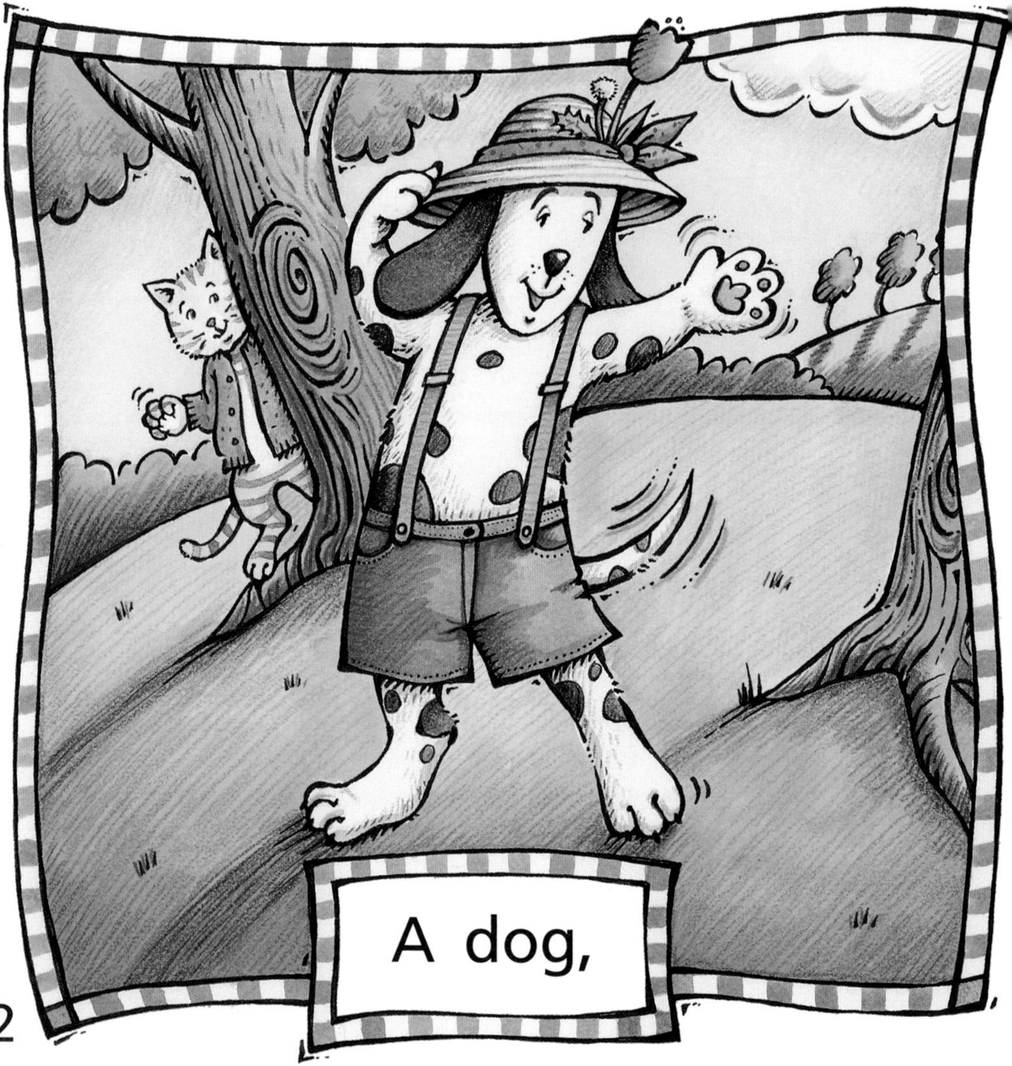

A dog,

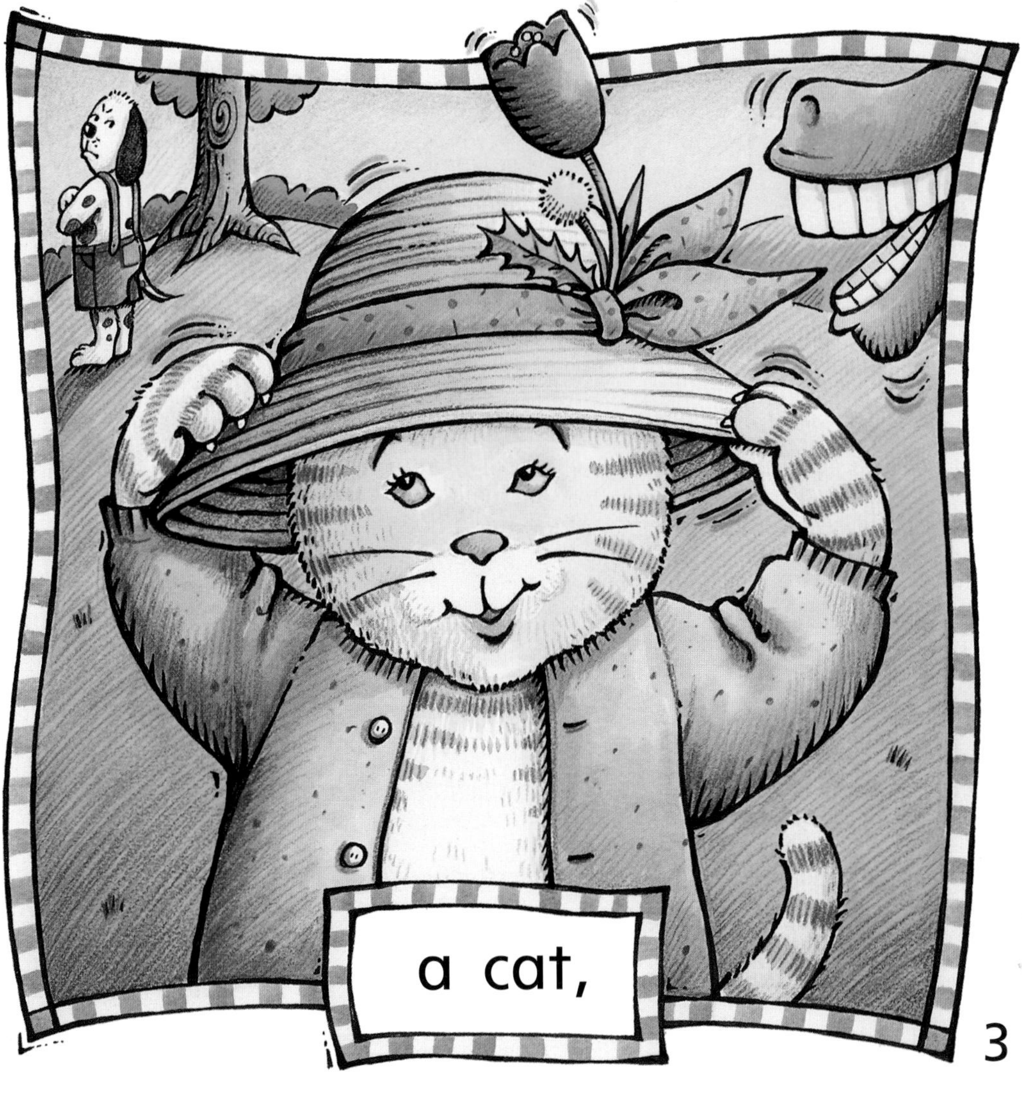

a cat,

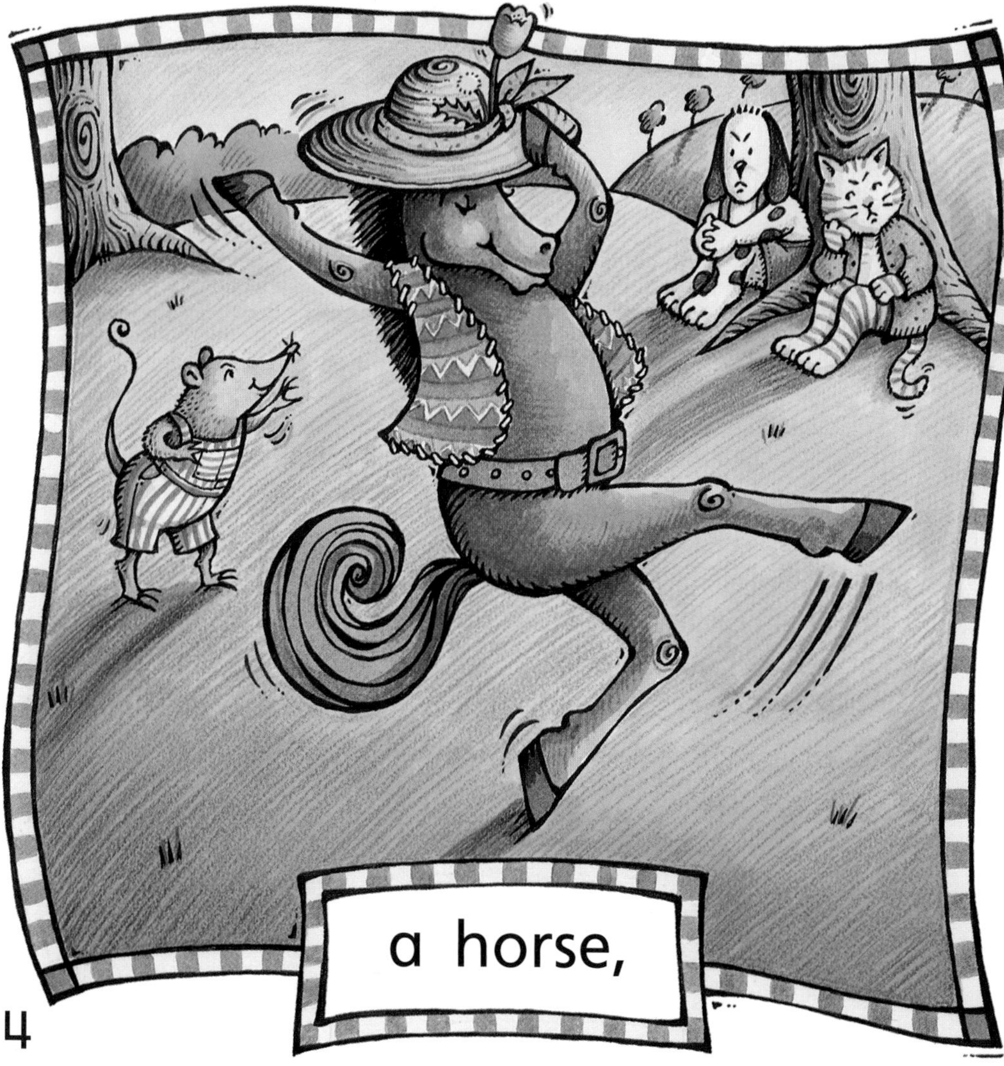

a horse,

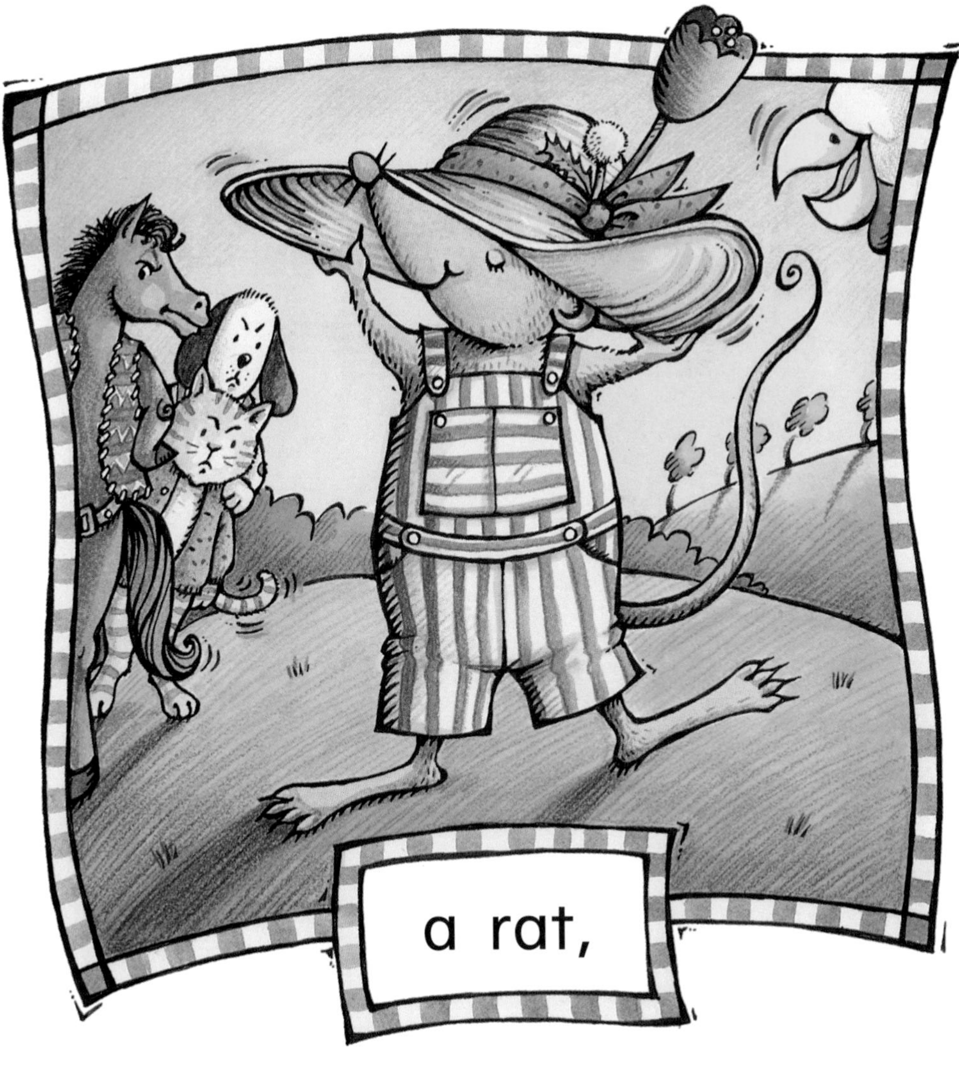

a rat,

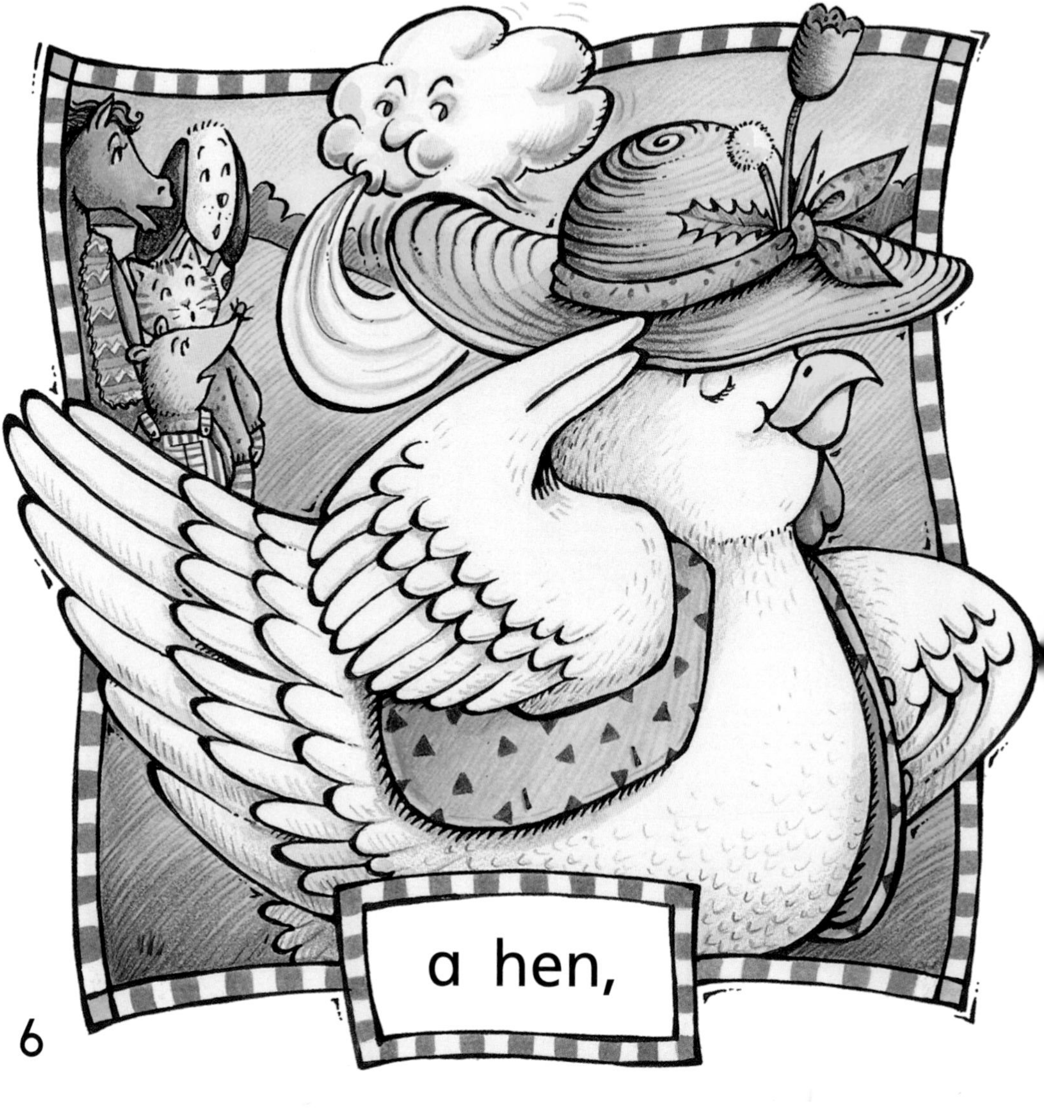

a hen,

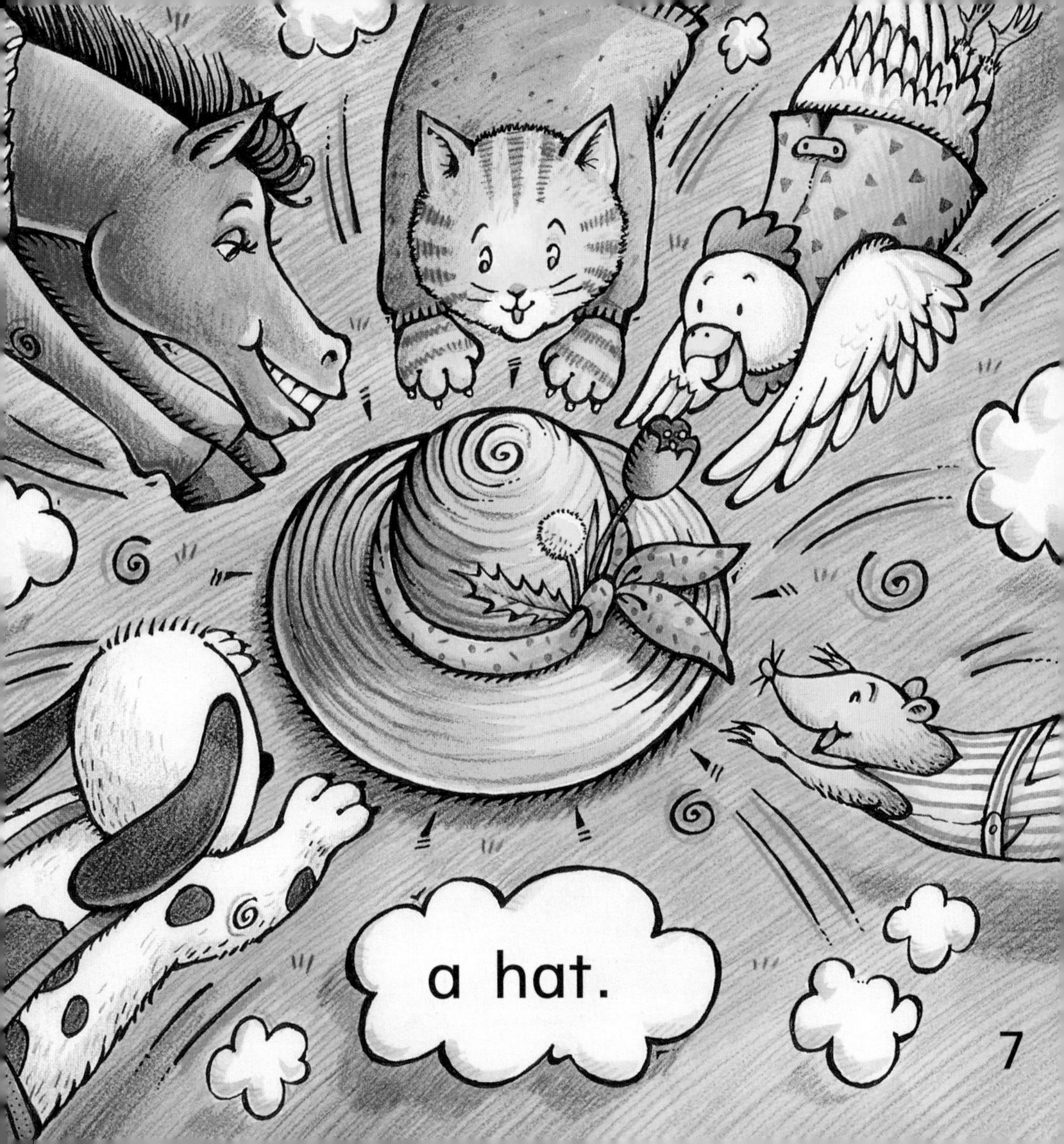

a hat.

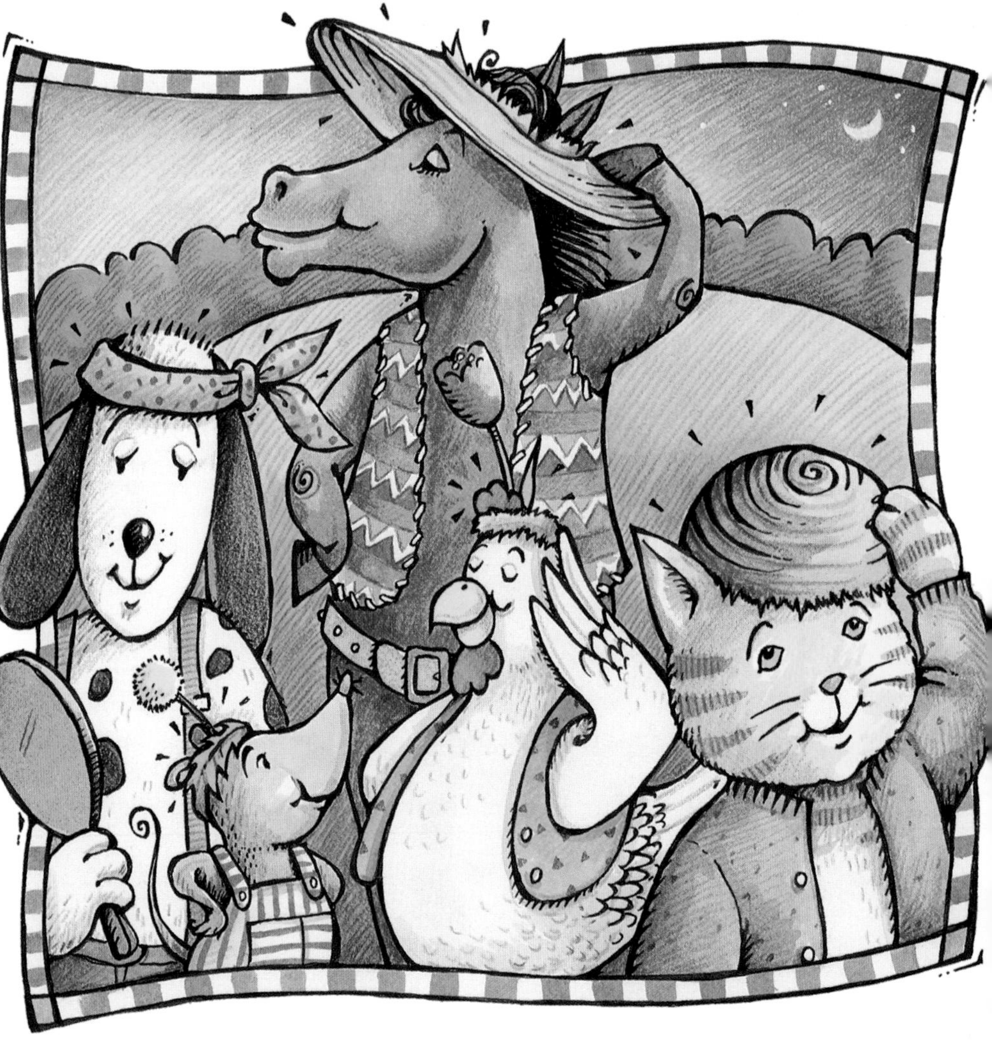